INCREDIBLE ANIMAL LIFE CYCLES

# LIFE CYCLE OF A
# BUTTERFLY

by Karen Latchana Kenney

pogo

# Ideas for Parents and Teachers

Pogo Books let children practice reading informational text while introducing them to nonfiction features such as headings, labels, sidebars, maps, and diagrams, as well as a table of contents, glossary, and index.

Carefully leveled text with a strong photo match offers early fluent readers the support they need to succeed.

## Before Reading

- "Walk" through the book and point out the various nonfiction features. Ask the student what purpose each feature serves.
- Look at the glossary together. Read and discuss the words.

## Read the Book

- Have the child read the book independently.
- Invite him or her to list questions that arise from reading.

## After Reading

- Discuss the child's questions. Talk about how he or she might find answers to those questions.
- Prompt the child to think more. Ask: Have you ever seen a butterfly come out of a chrysalis? Would you like to see an incredible event like that again?

Pogo Books are published by Jump!
5357 Penn Avenue South
Minneapolis, MN 55419
www.jumplibrary.com

Copyright © 2019 Jump!
International copyright reserved in all countries.
No part of this book may be reproduced in any form without written permission from the publisher.

Library of Congress Cataloging-in-Publication Data

Names: Kenney, Karen Latchana, author.
Title: Life cycle of a butterfly / by Karen Latchana Kenney.
Description: Minneapolis, MN: Jump!, Inc., [2018]
Series: Incredible animal life cycles | Includes index.
Audience: Ages 7-10.
Identifiers: LCCN 2017044914 (print)
LCCN 2017046651 (ebook)
ISBN 9781624968051 (e-book)
ISBN 9781624968037 (hardcover : alk. paper)
ISBN 9781624968044 (pbk.)
Subjects: LCSH: Butterflies—Life cycles—Juvenile literature.
Caterpillars—Juvenile literature.
Classification: LCC QL544.2 (ebook)
LCC QL544.2 .K465 2018 (print) | DDC 595.78/9156—dc23
LC record available at https://lccn.loc.gov/2017044914

Editor: Jenna Trnka
Book Designer: Molly Ballanger

Photo Credits: BarbaraKrupaPl/Shutterstock, cover (left); jps/Shutterstock, cover (right), 16 (top); tcareob72/Shutterstock, 1; Matee Nuserm/Shutterstock, 3; Tim UR/Shutterstock, 4 (leaves); IrinaK/Shutterstock, 4 (butterfly), 14-15; Sari ONeal/Shutterstock, 5, 11; blickwinkel/Alamy, 6-7; Jeffrey Moore/Shutterstock, 8-9; Gilbert S Grant/Getty, 10; Leena Robinson/Shutterstock, 12-13; StevenRussellSmithPhotos/Shutterstock, 16 (bottom); Buddy Mays/Getty, 17; SKLA/Getty, 18-19; Tommy Daynjer/Shutterstock, 20-21; Nikola Spasensoski/Shutterstock, 23.

Printed in the United States of America at Corporate Graphics in North Mankato, Minnesota.

# TABLE OF CONTENTS

# CHAPTER 1

## A NEW BUTTERFLY

Underneath a leaf, something wriggles out of a hard case. Its wings are colorful.

This new butterfly needs wings to fly from flower to flower. But this insect starts life without wings. It changes as it grows. Each change is one part of the butterfly's incredible life cycle.

Butterflies begin life as tiny eggs. These eggs are stuck to leaves. Each egg holds a growing caterpillar. A caterpillar is a butterfly **larva**.

A larva chews its way out of an egg when it is ready. Now it has one thing to do. Eat! It eats its eggshell. What else? The plant it grew on, too!

eggshell

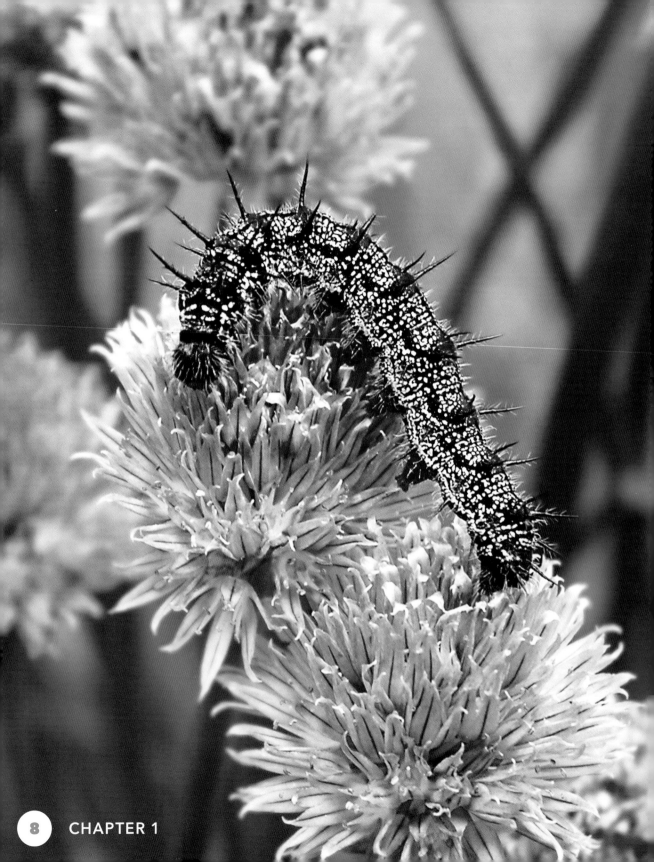

Caterpillars come in many colors. They can be fuzzy or hairy, spiky or smooth. All have tube-shaped bodies. They move by inching along. They find food so they can grow and change again.

## DID YOU KNOW?

Caterpillars have **spinnerets**. These release silk. Caterpillars use silk as a safety line. It keeps them from falling from plants.

# CHAPTER 2

## A CHANGING CATERPILLAR

As a caterpillar grows, its skin gets too tight. So what does it do? It **molts**. It sheds its old skin.

skin

A caterpillar molts a few times as it grows. It will sometimes eat its old skin. Soon it is ready for a bigger change.

The caterpillar sticks itself to a twig or leaf. It molts again. Its new skin forms a hard case. It is called a **chrysalis**.

The insect is now a **pupa**. It grows wings, legs, a mouth, and more. It stays safe inside its chrysalis.

**DID YOU KNOW?**

Inside the chrysalis, the caterpillar's body becomes mostly liquid. Then it starts growing its new body.

chrysalis ·····▶

When the adult is done growing, the chrysalis starts to break open. The butterfly pushes itself out. But it cannot fly yet.

First it pumps a liquid into its wings. It expands its wings. Now the butterfly begins its life in the air.

# TAKE A LOOK!

Each butterfly goes through a life cycle. It has four **stages**:

**egg:**
A butterfly begins as an egg. An adult female lays eggs.

**larva:**
A tiny caterpillar **hatches** from the egg. It is now a larva.

**pupa:**
The large caterpillar forms a chrysalis. It is now a pupa.

**adult:**
An adult butterfly comes out of the chrysalis.

# CHAPTER 3

# A BUTTERFLY'S LIFE

Butterflies soar high with their large wings. Beautiful colors and patterns cover them. Butterflies fly to find flowers.

Flowers have sweet **nectar** for butterflies. To eat, the insect uncurls its long **proboscis**. It is a tube that is like a straw. It reaches deep into flowers.

proboscis

**Pollen** sticks to butterflies. They carry it with them as they fly. It sticks to other flowers they land on. This helps the plants make seeds.

**DID YOU KNOW?**

Some butterflies **migrate** when the weather changes. They fly long distances in fall or spring. They fly to warmer weather.

pollen

egg

After a butterfly finds a **mate**, the female lays eggs. She finds the plant her baby caterpillars will like to eat. Where does she stick her eggs? Under the plant's leaves. Or on its stems.

The caterpillars grow quickly. Soon they will hatch. The life cycle starts again.

# ACTIVITIES & TOOLS

## BUTTERFLY FLIPBOOK

A flipbook makes drawings come alive. Flipping the pages shows motion or changes. Make one that shows how a butterfly changes in its life cycle.

**What You Need:**

- sticky notes
- colored pencils or markers
- books or websites showing stages of a butterfly's life cycle

❶ Take a stack of sticky notes. On each note, draw part of a butterfly's life cycle.

❷ Look through this book to see pictures of different parts of the life cycle. Look in other books or on the Internet for pictures, too.

❸ Start on the last page of the sticky note pile. Draw the first part of the butterfly's life cycle. Add fun colors and be creative!

❹ Work your way to the top of the note pile. Draw different stages of the life cycle on each note.

❺ End at the top note with a butterfly flying away.

❻ Now flip through your flipbook. Start by showing the bottom page first. Watch as the butterfly changes!

# GLOSSARY

**chrysalis:** The hard outer layer that protects a pupa.

**hatches:** Breaks out of an egg.

**larva:** A wormlike insect in a stage between an egg and pupa.

**mate:** A male or female partner of a pair of animals.

**migrate:** To fly away at a certain time of year to live in another climate.

**molts:** Sheds old skin or coverings to grow bigger.

**nectar:** A sweet liquid in flowers that birds and insects drink.

**pollen:** Tiny grains in flowers that plants need to make seeds.

**proboscis:** A long hollow body part.

**pupa:** An insect in a stage between a larva and adult.

**spinnerets:** Organs that caterpillars and spiders use to make silk.

**stages:** Steps or periods of development.

# INDEX

# TO LEARN MORE

Learning more is as easy as 1, 2, 3.

1) Go to www.factsurfer.com

2) Enter "lifecycleofabutterfly" into the search box.

3) Click the "Surf" button to see a list of websites.

With factsurfer, finding more information is just a click away.